KNOW WHO YOU ARE

Maria Yakubu

DEDICATION

This book is dedicated firstly to God Almighty, the owner of my soul, who gave me the grace and the wisdom to write it.

It is also dedicated to my darling husband and my lovely and beloved children. God bless you all.

ACKNOWLEDGEMENTS

First and foremost, I would like to acknowledge God's faithfulness and mercy in my life to be able to realise my dream of writing a book in my lifetime.

I would like to thank my beloved family for their encouragement as well as the Noble Women Intercessory Assembly for their prayers.

I also sincerely appreciate Fay's Book Editing, who did the editing, and Mr. Samuel Yakubu, who designed the book cover.

God bless you all in Jesus' Name.

Table of Contents

INTRODUCTION

This book is to encourage you to find out your God-given identity and show you a few steps on how to do that. Knowing who you are will help you stay focused on whatever you are doing in life. It might be your business, ministry, or education.

Know that you cannot fall or fail except if you accept it and stay there. Even if or when you fall or fail, get up and start again. With prayers, God will lift your hands.

1
KNOW YOUR GOD

It is not enough to know that the God of Abraham, Isaac, and Jacob exists. You need to have a personal relationship with Him. You need to know him as your father. When you know God for yourself, He shows up for you, meets you at the point of your needs, and gives your life a new purpose: His purpose.

People that know God for themselves communicate with Him through what we call "prayer." Communication, as we know it, is the exchange of information between entities. When I pass across a piece of information to you, I am certain you have received that information when you respond. The same thing goes for prayer! It has to be a conversation between you and God. It is a problem if God is speaking to you and you cannot hear Him. God speaks to us through several means and you will need to find out how he speaks to you. It could be a voice from within, or it could be through dreams (a vision shown to you while you are sleeping).

So when Joseph woke up, he married Mary, as the angel of the Lord had told him to.

(Matthew 1:24)

The confirmation Joseph needed came through a dream. What did you hear God say about your marriage? Did you hear Him say that you can have a blissful marriage but you need to stop that quarrel? Did you hear Him say that your finances will improve and that you should not give up? Did you hear Him say that if you keep praying, he will come to your house and turn things around? Did you hear Him say that you can have as many children as you want? Did you hear Him say that your future spouse is on the way? Did you hear Him say that you can have your own house and car(s)? Did you hear Him say that if you commit your life and surrender totally, He can keep you from any power of darkness tormenting your life and destiny? Did you hear him say that he is God and that nothing is impossible for Him?

He can fight and fight to the finish. He is the keeper of your soul. He did not fail the children of Israel. He has never failed, and He will not start with you. Trust God and He will invite you to a meeting.

"Come now, and let us reason together," Says the LORD, "Though your sins are like scarlet, They shall be as white as snow; Though they are red like crimson, They shall be as wool.

(Isaiah 1:18, NKJV)

Without instruction from God, you remain confused, without direction, and you walk in disobedience because you cannot obey an instruction you didn't receive. Did you hear Him say "go to Lagos" but you are going to Sokoto? What you hear matters!

Let me share my little story: This happened during the Kaduna state sharia crisis of 2000. I lived in Kaduna with my kids while my husband was in Abuja. I heard the Lord clearly. He said to me, "Come, let me take you out of this place." Then, I saw a mighty hand as large as a building take my hand while I held my children with my other hand. We stood on his palm, which looked like a house, and I found myself in Dutse Junction, Abuja. Before us was a river, and we walked past it. The Lord then said, "Go this way and I will make you one of those that succeed where I am taking you."

When we came to Abuja, we moved into an apartment in Kubwa, which was the accommodation of the company where my husband worked. Three different families were living in this three-bedroom house. When the time came for us to look for a house, my husband was led to Dutse Alhaji, and he got a place. It was time for us to move, and I heard the Lord directing us differently, and I said, "This is the way God is leading me." God gradually began to transform it into my Promised Land. This is my story.

What did you hear about your life, marriage, school, business, destiny, or career? I say to you, hold on to it! It may not look like it right now, but God is going to turn the situation around if you do not give up. God still speaks. The question is, do you listen to Him?

God can speak to you when you are walking down

the road, in your room, or even in a dream. I pray God gives you the grace to hear and see. God spoke to Joseph in a dream, but if he had not heard the voice of God, the outcome would have been disastrous.

God said, "I am who I am. You must tell them: 'The one who is called I AM has sent me to you.' Tell the Israelites that I, the LORD, the God of their ancestors, the God of Abraham, Isaac and Jacob, have sent you to them. This is my name forever; this is what all future generations are to call me. Go and gather the leaders of Israel together and tell them that I, the LORD, the God of their ancestors, the God of Abraham, Isaac and Jacob, appeared to you. Tell them that I have come to them and have seen what the Egyptians are doing to them. I have decided that I will bring them out of Egypt, where they are being treated cruelly, and will take them to a rich and fertile land – the land of the Canaanites, the Hittites, the Amorites, the Perizzites, the Hivites, and the Jebusites."

(Exodus 3:14-17)

God can change our circumstances to get us from where we are now to where He wants us to be in life. When you know God and recognise Him, He comes in and stops every prolonged battle. If you know God, there is nothing He cannot do for you.

He can also speak to us when we are awake like He spoke to Manoah's wife.

The Israelites sinned against the Lord again, and he let the Philistines rule them for forty years. At that time there was a man named Manoah from the town of Zorah. He was a member of the tribe of Dan. His wife had never been able to have children. The Lord's angel appeared to her and said, "You have never been able to have children, but you will soon be pregnant and have a son. Be sure not to drink any wine or beer, or eat any forbidden food; and after your son is born, you must never cut his hair, because from the day of his birth he will be dedicated to God as a Nazirite. He will begin the work of rescuing Israel from the Philistines."

(Judges 13:1-5)

Even in this generation, God is still speaking to his children and visiting them. Every believer should have this experience because it is a blessing when God visits you. Of course, as a believer, you have the Holy Spirit, so what do I mean by God "visiting you?" God can decide to send an angel to you, or you could experience an angelic ministration through a human being, but you need to position yourself to receive the message with clarity. You position yourself when you dwell in the place of prayer, when you are constantly edified as you go to church, when you serve in the church, when you preach the good news of salvation, and when you show the love of God to everyone.

It is not difficult to identify the voice of someone you know. When you hear your friend's voice, you can easily tell that it is your friend talking because you know that voice. The same goes for God. If you know God, when he speaks to you, you will surely recognise His voice because you have known him as a Father.

My sheep listen to my voice; I know them, and they follow me.

(John 10:27)

It is a wise thing to follow God. If you follow the voice of a stranger, you may be led astray, but God will never lead you astray. He said,

"...I will never leave you nor forsake you."

(Hebrews 13:5 NKJV)

So seek the face of God in whatever you do. Even Jesus Christ sought the face of God in his earthly assignment.

He went a little farther on, threw himself face downward on the ground, and prayed, "My Father, if it is possible, take this cup of suffering from me! Yet not what I want, but what you want."

(Matthew 26:39)

If Jesus Christ, the Son of the Most High God, can seek the face of God about His situation, what makes you think you can succeed on your own without God in that situation? Seek God's face like the woman with the issue of blood, and God will come through for you in every aspect of your life, in Jesus' Name!

According to Matthew 26:39, Jesus Christ threw

Himself face down on the ground. How do you approach God? You cannot come to God with arrogance and expect Him to assist you. You would also not approach a man with a negative attitude if you needed something from him. Some of us stand with our hands in our pockets, talking to God. People chew gum or are on the phone because the person they are talking to cannot wait, so God should hold on until they're done talking to whoever. Then they come back and say, "Yes, so where were we?" We see the position Christ took when praying; it was one of humility and reverence. I pray that if we have misbehaved in the place of prayer in any way, God will forgive us, draw us closer, and teach us how to approach Him. Amen.

Prayer Points

1. Lord, help me to know you more.
2. Lord, reveal yourself to me.
3. Through me, let my generation know you.

2

FELLOWSHIP

Fellowship is the connection or affiliation between a group of people that share the same interests or goals. It is a friendship or a connection that exists between people. Fellowship could also be a spiritual communion with a divine being.

Fellowship is very important in our lives. Every believer that is close to God fellowships with Him consistently. As a believer, it is important to understand that God does not have favourites; He loves us all equally. He made the sun that shines on everyone and the rain that falls on everyone. This shows how unconditional

God's love is. So, whatever it is we are going through, we need to know without any doubt that God loves us. It has to become a consciousness because it is our reality, and with this consciousness, we can flow with God more effectively.

An effective way to initiate this fellowship with God is by going on a retreat. As Christians, retreats are important for us, and it means taking some time to focus only on God. It slows you down and allows God to direct you and show you what to do. We see an example of this in the life of Jacob. He sent his family ahead of him to have a personal encounter with God. Things don't catch you by surprise when you do this.

For you to make the most out of your retreat, there are steps you need to put in place:

1. **Set goals:** Be specific when you set goals. What results do you want? Do you need direction? Do you need provision or healing? Not all paths are yours to follow, so write down your expectations, present them to God, and they will come to pass to the glory of God.

2. **Study the Bible:** Make a plan to study God's word.

You can even use a Bible reading plan to finish reading your Bible, and the Lord will strengthen you.

3. **Worship:** Create time to worship God and bring down His glory because the glory of God will give revelation, joy, and peace. When worship goes up, the blessings of the Lord come down and your heart desires will be granted. Create time to worship Him because He is your maker. That is the only thing he takes from you: WORSHIP.

4. **Prayer:** As a believer, we need to create time to pray because prayer is communicating with your maker. Tell Him what you want and how you want it.

"Come now, and let us reason together," Says the Lord, "Though your sins are like scarlet, They shall be as white as snow; Though they are red like crimson, They shall be as wool.

(Isaiah 1:18 NKJV)

Come reason with your maker and every issue in your life will be settled as you pray.

As you make these plans, you must walk in faith.

Faith goes hand in hand with the plans you make, but you need to have expectations, otherwise what exactly are you having faith for?

God wants you to hold on to Him and believe Him in whatever situation you are facing right now because as long as there is life, there is hope.

But anyone alive in the world of the living has some hope; a live dog is better off than a dead lion.

(Ecclesiastes 9:4)

This means that God is aware of what you are going through, whether sickness, poverty, affliction, trouble, or battle. You have presented it to Him in the place of fellowship in prayer and by studying His word. So, there is hope because you have not given up.

There is hope for a tree that has been cut down; it can come back to life and sprout. Even though its roots grow old, and its stump dies in the ground, with water it will sprout like a young plant.

(Job 14:7-9)

Jesus is the water of life, and as you fellowship with Him, He waters you and every part of your life that was withered. That business, career, and destiny will be brought back to life, both physically and spiritually.

Like I said before, make going on retreats a habit. A lot of us find it difficult to retreat, but it is so important in our walk with God.

Eagles take some time out to stay alone and take away all their old feathers. They wait for the new ones to grow so they can fly high. This is how a Christian ought to live. Practice staying alone with God to refresh your spiritual life.

Fellowship connects you to God and gives you spiritual eyes and ears. God wants you to be like Him. Remember, we were created in his image and likeness. Fellowship with Him protects you from everything in your life that does not look like Him. He purifies you and conforms you to His image so you can be an ambassador of Christ – a Christ representer!

Another thing fellowship does is that it strengthens your relationship with God; it makes you love Him even more. He reveals things to you in the place of fellowship that you would not have known if you were not fellowshipping with Him. The closer you are to a king, the more you learn about him and his kingdom.

Fellowship births revelation and kills fear. Fear does not exist when you are in the presence of God and are conscious of it. What could you possibly be afraid of when you are in the presence of the Mighty Man in Battle? Little children are known to be bolder and challenge their fears when they are in the presence of their parents. They have the boldness to challenge that uncle or aunt who has been threatening them. You may have heard a child say something like, "My Daddy will beat you for me." That is how you should face situations! You have God, your Father, a great defender, a protector, a deliverer, and a saviour. He is everything you need in life, and all you need to do is run to Him confidently and with boldness because He can do all things.

Leave all your worries with him, because he cares for you.

(1 Peter 5:7)

Prayer is the key that unlocks closed doors. Never stop praying, no matter how dark and hopeless the situation may be. Maintain your faith in Christ Jesus, and He will handle the situation for you. When you sweat in the place of prayer, the Lord fights your battles. When you pray effectively, you see results. We, as believers, need to stay in the place of prayer and fellowship with God. Without that, we do not have direction, and without direction, we are left confused and led astray.

This is my testimony. In 2002, I was pregnant and praying for a safe delivery like any other pregnant woman would. Then, I had a dream. In this dream, I went out fishing. It took me a long time, but I was finally able to catch one fish. I stood there admiring this fish, and before I knew it, the fish slipped from my hands and fell back into the river. I wailed and asked God why this happened, and I heard a very loud voice. It said, "Prepare for a battle." I replied, "God, I do not know how to fight. You are the only one that can fight and fight to finish. God, fight for me." Then I woke up.

I knew there was going to be a battle, but I also knew that my God is a Mighty Man of War, so I continued praying and started to fast. Three days later, on December 25, 2002, I went into labour and I gave birth to a baby girl, which was my heart's desire. She was born with chronic jaundice, which the hospital started to treat immediately. Three days passed, and her body became very weak, to the point where she could no longer suck my breast. We rushed her back to the hospital where we met with the doctor. The doctor said that nothing could be done and that the medicine administered to her was exactly what she needed to get better. But she was not responding positively to it. "Just take her home," the doctor said. I remembered the dream I had and I told God that I could not do this without Him.

I took my baby home, locked my door, and I said to God, "The doctor might not know what to do, but you know what to do. So come through for me, Lord Jesus. You are the doctor of all doctors, and you are my God. I know you are still in the business of healing and deliverance. You delivered me when my enemies wanted to take my life while I was in labour during the pregnancy of my third child. You healed my son when he was sick. Lord, you never change and I know you will do this for me."

I had prayed for an hour and a half when I heard a voice say, "Raise your hands." I did so and continued praying. Ten minutes later, God said, "Lay your hands on the baby." Immediately, I laid my hands on her. It was like an electric shock and she started to cry. This was a baby that could not cry or suck her mother's breast. I rushed her back to the hospital, and the doctor asked me what I did to her. I told the doctor that I prayed, and he said, "Madam, go back and pray more because as it is now, there is nothing we can do." My child lived. We named her "Kindness," because the Lord truly showed us an act of kindness by bringing her back to life.

I pray for you that the Lord will bring back your baby! Your baby could be your child, your business, ministry, finance, career, political power, or destiny. Whatever it is that was dead in your life, the Lord will revive it in Jesus' name. He will bring it back to life. All hope is never lost. Always believe that God can bring you out of that situation.

What is your doctor saying concerning that sickness or child delay? Whatever it is, don't give up. Take it to the Lord in prayer. He did it for me when it seemed like all hope was lost in the hospital in 2002, and He will do it for you. That is who God is and He will never change.

Do you remember the story of the Shunamite

woman?

He closed the door and prayed to the Lord. Then he lay down on the boy, placing his mouth, eyes, and hands on the boy's mouth, eyes, and hands. As he lay stretched out over the boy, the boy's body started to get warm. Elisha got up, walked around the room, and then went back and again stretched himself over the boy. The boy sneezed seven times and then opened his eyes. Elisha called Gehazi and told him to call the boy's mother. When she came in, he said to her, "Here's your son."

(1 Kings 4:33-36)

That is our God! His name is Jehovah Rapha, the God that heals. Never allow your present situation to determine your future. Know what you want and tell God in the place of fellowship. Never think God has forgotten you. He will never forget you, and He is calling you to live your life for Him.

Some may say they are not graduates or they are women which is why they are unable to do all that they are supposed to do. I encourage you to do the little you can and God will lift you. On the last day, we will all stand before God. The husband will stand alone, the wife will stand alone, and the children will stand alone. God is not going to give you a straight pass to heaven because you are a woman. Everyone will be judged accordingly.

Some women made an impact in the Bible. One of them is Deborah.

Now Deborah, the wife of Lappidoth, was a prophet, and she was serving as a judge for the Israelites at that time. She would sit under a certain palm tree between Ramah and Bethel in the hill country of Ephraim, and the people of Israel would go there for her decisions. One day she sent for Barak son of Abinoam from the city of Kedesh in Naphtali and said to him, "The Lord, the God of Israel, has given you this command: 'Take ten thousand men from the tribes of Naphtali and Zebulun and lead them to Mount Tabor. I will bring Sisera, the commander of Jabin's army, to fight you at the Kishon River. He will have his chariots and soldiers, but I will give you victory over him.'" Then Barak replied, "I will go if you go with me, but if you don't go with me, I won't go either." She answered, "All right, I will go with you, but you won't get any credit for the victory, because the Lord will hand Sisera over to a woman." So Deborah set off for Kedesh with Barak.

(Judges 4:4-9)

In Judges 4:17-22, God also used another woman named Jael, the wife of Hebar, to give victory to the children of Israel. There is also Esther, who God used to give victory to the Jews. I pray you will be the next man or woman that God will use for your family, state, and nation. In that same country, there were men of valour, but in this case, God decided to use a woman. God can use anybody. You just have to avail yourself and the Lord will use you to His glory.

Prayer Points

1. O Lord, show me mercy in any way I have neglected your work.
2. Any power limiting the grace of God in my life, let go.
3. Any power contending with the power of God in my life is a liar. I am victorious in Jesus' Name.

4. Oh Lord my God, heal me from any sickness and disease in Jesus' Name.

5. Any coffin calling my name to the grave, you are a liar. I refuse to die in Jesus' Mighty Name.

6. O God, arise and defend your name in my life, family, and ministry in Jesus' Name.

7. Oh Lord, draw me closer to you.

8. Lord, open my spiritual eyes and ears so that I may see and hear you loud and clear when you speak to me.

9. O Lord, move me forward in Jesus' Name.

10. Lord, resurrect my spiritual strength, ministry, business, or any other endeavour that is dead in Jesus' Name.

3

FOCUS

To focus is to fix your attention on something or someone. If you want to do well in life, work, business, ministry, and family, you need to be focused. Refuse to be distracted. In short, CONCENTRATE!

There are thousands of things out there fighting for your attention. These things keep you from hitting your targets. They are called distractions. If you want God's attention in your life, ministry, and destiny, you need to be focused. If you stay with the word of God and fix your eyes on Jesus, you will see the glory of God.

Focus on God, stay with his word, and stay in the church because the presence of God will move you to the level you want to be in life.

Beware! Distraction is a disease that throws men into a pit called confusion. When you are in a state of confusion, you lose direction, and when you lose direction, you are no longer focused on God. You find yourself bitter, focusing on everything that is not going well, constantly nagging and complaining about who did and who didn't do what. Slowly, pride can set in, and before you know it, you find it difficult to pray or do anything for that matter. That is exactly what the devil wants. He wants us distracted and unable to do the work of God, but that is not what God wants for us. In Jesus' Name, I pray that you will not miss the will of God for you.

When you are focused, you can successfully eliminate doubt and fear. Receive boldness from the Lord and walk in it. Embrace challenges. Reject negative thoughts and words from people telling you that you are not good enough. Believe in yourself and know that you are just as good as any other person on the planet.

Life may not be going the way you want it to, but

God is always good and faithful. You might not have built your dream house or bought your dream car, but God is still good. You may not have found your dream girl or the tall, dark, and handsome man you want, but guess what? God is still good! You may be seeking admission into the university, a job, or an opportunity to travel abroad and haven't gotten it yet, but God is good and faithful. Life may be dishing out frustration and hopeless situations to you, but God is good and He remains faithful. You just have to fix your eyes on Him. You have to be focused and very soon you will see the glory of God. Sing a new song and dance the dance of a winner. God is faithful and will always play his part. The question is, are you playing yours? Avoid distractions and pray to Him at your prayer altar daily. He is a covenant-keeping God.

You do not need anybody to tell you before you believe that you are good enough. You just need to believe that you are a great warrior who is ready to fight your way to the top and move on, no matter the circumstances. Listen, never allow thoughts from the devil to bring you down. Your present condition, your background, educational qualifications, or your neighbourhood do not define you. People may try to intimidate you, but always remember that God is on your side and will do for you what no man on earth can. When he lifts you, no one can bring you down. So, always commit your ways to him in prayers and He will uphold you.

Never depend on people for success and breakthroughs. Depend only on God. Talk to God and He will place it in the heart of men to favour you. Even when you are granted favour by men, recognise the power of God that touched their hearts to bless you. Always trust God in your situation, and He will see you through, answer your prayers, and give you a testimony. I pray for you that any altar standing between you and your success is set ablaze and burnt to ashes in the name of Jesus!

In anything you do, stand firm and be focused. Do not be discouraged or give up because the Lord, your Rewarder and Redeemer, sees and knows everything.

Do you have a vision? Have you ever heard a voice that said to you, "Go and preach the gospel" or seen in a vision or a dream someone giving you instructions? Have you seen yourself leading prayers? That is a sign that God is calling you and wants you to do something for Him. Get ready. Look for a good mentor and undergo training because God wants to use you.

I looked for someone who could build a wall, who could stand in the places where the land has crumbled and defend the land when my anger is about to destroy it, but I could find no one.

(Ezekiel 22:30)

I believe you will allow God to use you in his kingdom. I pray that God will grant you ears to listen so you can hear Him when He speaks, because what you hear matters. When you hear, make sure you are hearing the right thing. You can do this by staying with God's word so you become more familiar with his voice. When you do this, you will be able to distinguish your voice from God's voice. You may think you are unqualified, but God still wants you! He is going to guide you and teach you all that you need to know. Get ready!

You may say, "Oh, but I'm not a graduate," but the Lord says, "Come." You may say, "I am not a pastor, an evangelist, or a bishop," but the Lord says, "Come." You may say, "I am not a good singer," but the Lord says, "Come." You may say, "But I don't even know how to do anything," but the Lord says, "Come."

The Kingdom of God is big, the harvest is large, and every one of us can fit in, so come! Wherever your place of service is, serve wholeheartedly. Your service might not be noticed by men, but the God you serve knows and He sees, so serve Him faithfully. You may say, "I do not know where to serve." Well, this is a personal invitation. If you are from Edo state, search for Etsako Christian Association (ECA) from wherever you are in Nigeria. You can serve God there by taking the word of God to your people in Edo state. There are other ministries just like this one, so find one and be a part of what God is doing. Also, look for a Bible-believing church to serve in, and God will make you a marvel in the eyes of men.

One reliable way to improve your focus is to write down your visions and revelations.

...Write down clearly on tablets what I reveal to you, so that it can be read at a glance. Put it in writing, because it is not yet time for it to come true. But the time is coming quickly, and what I show you will come true. It may seem slow in coming, but wait for it; it will certainly take place, and it will not be delayed.

(Habakkuk 2:2-3)

As you wait for the promises of God to manifest in your life, keep praying and fasting, loving the people around you, and helping in every little way you can. It should never get to the point where you start to compare yourself with others. Do not imitate what you see other people doing, but rather do what God has assigned you to do for Him. God has already set a goal for you, so do not miss your target. I pray that as you remain focused, God will take away every hindrance, stronghold, stumbling block, and reproach that plans to stop you from carrying out your God-given assignment. For you to fight reproach, you need to practise the Word of God daily. In other words, put it into action.

In conclusion, my friends, fill your minds with those things that are good and that deserve praise: things that are true, noble, right, pure, lovely and honourable. Put into practice what you learned and received from me, both from my words and from my actions. And the God who gives us peace will be with you

(Philippians 4:8-9)

Every plan of the enemy to distract you, wherever

they gather to plan, they will never agree and they will scatter in Jesus' Name! Amen.

The Word of God is power. It is your weapon of war against the enemy. The Word of God will defend, protect, and liberate you.

I keep your law in my heart, so that I will not sin against you.

(Psalm 119:11)

The more of God's Word you know, the more powerful you are, and the abundance of God's grace will continually rest on you. Every plan devised by the enemy to bring you down, both physically and spiritually, will fail miserably and disgracefully. The Word of God is the most powerful weapon or tool any child of God could have in their possession. As believers, we should cherish the Word of God. We should study the Word of God with fervency so that the distractions of this world will not take it from us. Not studying the Word of God leaves you empty, naked, and vulnerable to the attacks of the enemy. The Word of God, I say again, is a cover.

Our Lord and Saviour Jesus Christ used the Word of God to overcome the devil in the wilderness. So, when you are in the wilderness of your life, you also need the Word of God to overcome. In that situation, struggle, pain, or issue in life, the Lord will help you to overcome it all in Jesus' Mighty Name.

I am not saying that you should only be familiar with Bible verses. No! Even the devil spoke from the scriptures at some point. Remember, he was once an angel before pride cost him his position. As a child of God, the Word of God must dwell richly in you. You have to be rooted in the Word of God, and this happens not just by quoting the Bible but by doing all that it requires of you.

Whatever the Lord asks you to do that will bring Him glory, do it! You are not reading this book right now by accident. I pray the Lord makes a name for Himself through you in Jesus' Name. God will continue to help you. Amen.

Prayer Points

1. Lord, help me not to be distracted. Help me to focus on what you want for me.
2. Grant me divine direction.
3. Help me to work through my destiny.

4

DESTINY

Let us look at the meaning of the word "destiny." Destiny means that to which every person or thing is called. It is a predetermined state or condition ordained by divine or human will. This means that you have been programmed and fixed in God's divine calendar. He did not just fix you for no reason, but rather, He secured you for a purpose. I pray that you will fulfil your destiny in life. Many people have died without fulfilling their destinies in life but that is not your portion. On the other hand, many have escaped the trap of the enemy with God's help, and they were able to fulfil their destinies. An example is Joseph. The enemy tried to make sure that his dream, purpose, and destiny were destroyed, but God used all the devices of the enemy to hasten Joseph towards his destiny. I decree that God will use the devices of the enemy against you to help you fulfil your destiny.

God had a purpose for which He sent Joseph to Egypt ahead of his people. God knew that there was going to be a famine in the land of Canaan, and so He sent Joseph ahead of them. His brothers would have killed him, but God had not finished with him, so his brothers changed their minds. In the Mighty Name of Jesus, I pray for you that your enemies will change their minds that were filled with evil intentions for you. Even in your individual life, many might have tried to kill you several times, even when you were still in your mother's womb. But the owner of your soul kept you from their evil plots because there was a divine assignment for you to accomplish. That is why the evil plan of that Pharaoh in your family did not succeed.

Who is this Pharaoh? This Pharaoh is the enemy of your destiny who does not want anything good to happen to the children of destiny born into any family, and whether you believe it or not, this Pharaoh is in every family. The God who owns your life kept this Pharaoh from taking your life when you were still a baby, which means that there is a divine assignment you must fulfil. Locate that divine assignment now and get to work. Destiny is an important issue, so be careful not to sell this, your divine assignment, to the devil. After losing it, no amount of crying can bring it back. Value God's assignment in your life and work faithfully.

When we hear about great men and women in the Bible, they were not spirits but men and women like you and me who stood their ground and were faithful to believe what God spoke concerning them and they obeyed God's word to the end. The Bible says that:

But whoever holds out to the end will be saved.

(Matthew 24:13)

So, wait upon the Lord and follow His instructions. He will surely lead you through. Noah was destined to build an ark and he waited for a very long time, to the extent that people began to mock him and say all sorts of things to him, but because he knew he had been fixed in God's calendar, he waited and endured all the insults. He was called all kinds of names, but the name they called him was not the original name God gave him. The people later started coming and believing in him when the flood came, but it was too late for them, but Noah and his family were saved. I encourage you to stay focused. Do not listen to those mockers and do not do what they do or say what they say. Do not wear what they wear or even go where they go. You are so different from them. You are a person of destiny. So, wait upon the Lord, for He is near and He will come through for you. When he does, they will change the way they think about you, and very soon, God will use you to change their lives for the good.

Your family might not value you now but wait. Your neighbour, church, state, and country might be mocking, insulting, and devaluing you, but wait. The Lord will show up for you, spice you up, and those that look down on you will begin to look up to you. Focus on your goals and destiny. The Bible says:

Looking unto Jesus, the author and the finisher
of our faith ...

(Hebrews 12:2)

He is the only one who can change that situation

and take you from zero to wherever he wants you to be. Read the Bible and pray constantly because you need to know the One who formed you and you need to know Him well. When you fail or fall, don't be afraid to start over and over again. It doesn't matter how many times you fall; what matters is that when you fall, you do not remain on the floor, but you get up and stand tall. Take giant steps daily because that is what God wants you to do. He wants you to take that one step towards Him, and He will take ten steps towards you so that your destiny, like David's, will be greatly announced. Those midnight prayers you are afraid to start will announce you. Fasting, which you are hesitant to begin, will truly announce you. That Bible that you are afraid of reading from Genesis to Revelations can bring you out of the bush and into the palace. That battle that you are afraid to fight, and the Goliath you are hesitating to confront, might be what will deliver your visa into your hands. The gospel that you are not preaching to unbelievers is what will break the backbone of the enemy. The assignment that God is sending you on right now that you are afraid to do might be a channel to your heart's desire. The person you are not talking to right now might be the helper of your destiny. Now, get up, shake off the dust, and MOVE. He who called you will keep you and never leave you, nor forsake you.

Behold, He who keeps Israel shall neither slumber nor sleep

(Psalm 121:4, NKJV)

Walk with your shoulders raised in Christ Jesus. I know by now you are no longer afraid, so tell that situation that Jesus is here with you. If the devil could not kill you when you were still blood in your mother's womb or a baby knowing nothing, I tell you they cannot kill you now because God wants you to fulfil your divine destiny to the glory of God.

Never compare yourself to another person because your divine calling and anointing are not the same as theirs. Your assignments are different from any other person's, so focus on your divine assignment and you will fulfil your destiny because the person you are comparing yourself to might be sent to the north and you to the west. The work in the north is quite different from the work in the west, so when you compare yourself to another, you will end up doing another person's work and leave your place in destiny vacant.

Esther was in the palace to fulfil her destiny, and that was why her uncle Mordecai ran to her to take up the challenge of going to the king. She immediately got the message and said:

"Go and get all the Jews in Susa together; hold a fast and pray for me. Don't eat or drink anything for three days and nights. My servant women and I will be doing the same. After that, I will go to the king, even though it is against the law. If I must die for doing it, I will die."

(Esther 4:16)

Esther did not die, but rather God used her to save the children of Israel. What is it that you are afraid of? Take up the challenge, fast, and pray about it like Esther. Stand up and confront that evil in your house, family, ministry, business, education, marriage, and even in your country. Do not let the devil use the weapon of fear to stop you. Your family and country are waiting for you because you are destined to save them, as Esther and David did. In Jesus' Mighty Name, I pray for you that your destiny will not be wasted. Amen.

Prayer Points

1. Lord, I thank you for keeping me alive to see today.

2. Lord, show me mercy in Jesus' Mighty Name.

3. Lord, I surrender my life and destiny into your hands. Use me for Your glory in Jesus' Name.

4. Lord, because my destiny is in your hands, no one will use my destiny to shine except me, in Jesus' Name.

5. My destiny will not be wasted in Jesus' Name.

6. The destiny of my spouse and my children will arise and shine in Jesus' Name.

5

KNOW WHAT YOU WANT

If you don't know what you want, you will be beating around the bush, but if you know what you want and why you want it, you will not be pushed around. Knowing what you want is very important, but so is knowing why you want it. You should know why you want whatever it is that you want. In whatever you do for yourself or for God, your motives matter. If your motives are right, you will stay with what you want no matter the pressure or situation that might arise. Do hold onto what you want and do not give in to any side distraction. The two blind men knew what they wanted, and they did not let themselves get distracted.

Two blind men who were sitting by the road heard that Jesus was passing by, so they began to shout, "Son of David! Have mercy on us, sir!" The crowd scolded them and told them to be quiet. But they shouted even more loudly, "Son of David! Have mercy on us, sir!" Jesus stopped and called them. "What do you want me to do for you?" he asked them.

(Matthew 20:30-32)

The two blind men heard that Jesus was passing; what are you hearing in this period of COVID? What do you want to hear – the number of deaths or what Jesus is saying concerning COVID? What do you want – for COVID to end or to continue? Some are enjoying it, but some are not because they have no food, no money, no peace, and no comfort, so they are crying out like the two blind men calling on the Name of Jesus Christ for help, but those who are comfortable and have eyes to see are shutting them up because they are okay and can see. The world we are living in now is like that.

Don't let someone who doesn't know what you are

going through shut you up. Don't let those who are not in your shoes shut you up. Don't let those who can see when you cannot see shut you up. Don't let those who were born with a silver spoon in their mouths shut you up. Don't ever let people who feel that they are better, more educated, or wiser than you shut you up. This world that we are living in is like a class. Everybody good, bad, and ugly, is there. In the same class, some will come out with a first class, some with a second class, some with a third class, or operation-let-my-people-go (those who didn't do well enough to make a third class).

Do not let people who do not have the same vision as you shut you up. Have a strong conviction, and know what you want. If you do not give up, you will get it, and when you are victorious, those that were trying to shut you up and those that criticised you will celebrate and congratulate you later on. So, do not stop or give up until you are congratulated and celebrated, dear reader. Don't let your condition and situation put you down either, like the two blind men. They knew what they wanted and that was why they did not give up. Rather, they shouted even more, and Jesus stopped and asked them, "What do you want me to do for you?" Never ever let the opinion of others stop you. Go ahead and get married, go to school, start that ministry, and go for evangelism if God is leading you to. Do the work of the Master and He will do yours. Rise to be the king and queen that God has made you to be. Always remember, Jesus is with you.

Continue, my brothers and sisters, continue. Do not allow anything or anyone to stop you. Stand your ground and know exactly what you want. Jesus will stop for you and he will ask you what you want. I see you smiling and laughing. Jesus is very close to where you are now in your ministry, marriage, school, and business. Jesus is closer than you know. All you need to do is call him daily, call him anytime, and call him without ceasing. I see him stopping for you.

Tell Jesus what you want, as the blind men did.

"Sir," they answered, "We want you to give us our sight!" Jesus had pity on them and touched their eyes; at once they were able to see, and they followed him.

(Matthew 20:33-34)

That job, money, children, political power, or whatever you want, call Jesus's attention to it and He will give you what you want. But, remember to follow him even after you have gotten it, and the Lord will expand your borders as you continue to follow him. In this life, you must know what you want, how you want it, and be sure of your motives for wanting it. Hold on to it. If you don't, some people will take it from you and make you a slave to your vision. I pray that the Lord will turn to you quickly and deliver you from people that want to shut you up.

Let me tell you a bit more of my story. When I was much younger, I was going to the farm with my cousin, and I saw a ripe mango. I showed the beautiful ripe mango to my cousin, and he ran and picked it up and refused to give it to me no matter how much I cried and shouted, "Give me my mango." He refused to give it to me because I showed it to him first, instead of me taking it for myself. Do not sell your vision or allow someone else to take your place. You might not have the money yet, but don't sell your vision. You might think you are not qualified, but don't sell your vision. Hold on to it because Jesus will show up.

The vision you have is for an appointed time because the Bible tells me that it will surely come to pass.

"Then the LORD answered me and said: "Write the vision and make it plain on tablets, that he may run who reads it. For the vision is yet for an appointed time; but at the end it will speak, and it will not lie. Though it tarries, wait for it; because it will surely come, it will not tarry."

(Habakkuk 2:2-3 NKJV)

Don't ever underestimate yourself. You are a special breed. What has God placed in your heart? Hold on to it, nurture it, and call upon the name of the Lord. He will show up for you and you will smile.

Nurture that gift that God has given you and guard it jealously. In your secret place of prayer, call on God. The situation might not look good, but don't give up. Build an altar of prayer around it and leave it there at the altar with God Almighty. A day will come when He will call you or turn to you, as He did with the two blind men. "I don't have any money" is not an issue. "I don't know what to do" is not an issue. The issue is, do you know what you want to see? If you do, hold on to it and everything will be okay when God shows up.

Stop crying, stop regretting and let us pray these few

prayer points before we continue.

1. Lord, show me mercy and give me the vision to see where the solution to my problem is in Jesus' Name.

2. Lord, help me to take back what the enemy has stolen from my life and destiny.

3. Whatever I have lost during the period of the COVID-19 pandemic, by the power that is in the Name of Jesus, I recover it all in Jesus' Name.

4. Divine Holy Spirit, I commit my life into your hands. Please fight my battles in Jesus' Name.

5. The Lord God of Elijah that answers by fire, please answer all my prayer requests by fire.

6. Lord, open my eyes to see and know what you want me to do for you.

7. Empower me to do your will.

8. Thank you, Lord, for answering my prayers in Jesus' Name.

The two blind men told Jesus that they wanted to see, but they didn't tell him what they wanted to see. You can tell Jesus what you want to see. Let me list a few examples, and you can add to them anytime.

1. You want to see Him so you can know Him. If you don't see and know Him, you cannot serve Him well.
2. You want to see and know Him so that His power will be made manifest in your life and destiny.
3. You want to see Him so that you can point others to Him because you know Him.

As Christians, we need to cry out to God like the two blind men to show us mercy so that we can see both physically and spiritually. It is very important because if you cannot visualise, there are certain heights in life you may never be able to attain. If you can see, there are problems that you can avoid, but if you can't see, you will fall into those avoidable problems. In this case, seeing and knowing work hand in hand. It is what you see that you can know, and what you don't see, you may not know. God gave me this song.

I want to know you more

I want to know you, daddy

The God of my salvation

I want to know you, Lord

I know you want to see growth in your marriage, business, political life, ministry, evangelism, and prayer life and you want to see God expanding your territories. You want to see the glory of God manifested in your life, family, and ministry.

The worst thing that can happen to a believer is for him/her to be spiritually blind. They may not even be blind physically. You don't have to be a prophet before you can see spiritually. The Bible speaks about the signs that follow those who believe.

"Believers will be given the power to perform miracles: they will drive out demons in My Name..."

(Mark 16:17a)

No one can cast out an evil spirit if they are unable to see spiritually. As we journey through life as believers, we need to see so that we do not stumble in life. Say, "Lord, open my eyes so that I may see your glory and power." You cannot see if you have not given your life to Jesus Christ. Dear reader, you can do that right now by saying this short prayer.

Lord Jesus, thank you for the life you have given me.

Come into my life, be my Lord and Saviour. From now on, I surrender my life and destiny to you. So, take over my life. Satan, listen, today I break every covenant I have with you because I now have a new Master. His Name is Jesus Christ. Thank you, Jesus, for accepting me. AMEN.

Wow, you have just given your life to Jesus Christ. You are now a new creature. Old things have passed away, and everything has become new (1 Corinthians 5:17). You might not see the newness because it happens in your spirit. My brother and sister, I congratulate you. Look for a Bible-believing and practising church near you and get a Bible you can understand. Start to read from the gospel of John. God bless you in Jesus' Name. Amen

JESUS IS LORD!